HELEN

by Maureen Lennon

Helen was first developed as part of FUSE
at Leeds Playhouse and had a rehearsed reading
as part of their 2019 Furnace Festival.

It was first produced by Terrain and Theatre503, and
premiered at Theatre503, London, on 9 May 2023,
supported by Hull City Council, MG Futures, Sir James
Reckitt Charity and City Health Care Partnership.

HELEN

Cast

Helen	Jo Mousley
Becca	Chloe Wade

Creative Team

Writer	Maureen Lennon
Director	Tom Bellerby
Composer and Sound Designer	Jim Harbourne
Set & Costume Designer	Alice Hallifax
Lighting Designer	Joseph Ed Thomas

Production Team

Producer	Sarah Penney
Stage Manager (London)	Sarah Goodyear
Set Builder	Andy Ross

Thanks To

Jacqui Honess-Martin, who believed in this play and whose brilliant notes led to it finding its current form. To Sarah and Tom, who have worked tirelessly to make sure it happens and lent their talent, determination and friendship. To our gorgeous cast and creative team. To Giles Smart, who is the best agent and champion. To my biggest supporter, Declan McCann.

And to Richard Bean, Andrew Shepherd, Jessy Zschorn of Studio Blue Creative, Adam Pownall & the team at Hull Truck Theatre, Silent Uproar Productions, Middle Child Theatre, Wykeland Group Limited, Jamie Potter, sobananapenguin, Erin Anderson, Rio Matchett, Kelly Hotten and Norah Lopez Holden, who have all so generously played a part in *Helen*'s journey.

Maureen Lennon
Writer

Maureen is a Hull-based writer. She is a graduate from the English and Theatre Studies BA from the University of Bristol and the Writing for Performance and Publication MA from the University of Leeds (Distinction). She is an Associate Artist of Middle Child Theatre, a Leeds Playhouse FUSE writer 2019 and a Sphinx30 playwright. Her play *Helen* was shortlisted for the 2020 Theatre503 International Playwriting Award. In 2018 she was longlisted for the Alfred Bradley Bursary for Radio Drama. Her last play, *The Coppergate Woman* was produced by York Theatre Royal in 2022. Her play, *Us Against Whatever*, was produced in 2019 by Middle Child Theatre in association with Hull Truck Theatre and Liverpool Everyman & Playhouse. It is published by Oberon Books. Her play *Bare Skin On Briny Waters* (co-written with Tabitha Mortiboy) was produced by Bellow Theatre and Hull UK City of Culture in the 2017 Edinburgh Takeover and received two award commendations from NSDF. She has also written work for Paines Plough, Sheffield Theatres, Pilot Theatre and Hull Truck Theatre. She is currently under commission to Silent Uproar, Hull Truck Theatre & Pilot Theatre and Middle Child Theatre.

Tom Bellerby
Director

Tom is a theatre director, dramaturg and co-chair of Pilot Theatre. He has previously been the Resident Director at the Donmar Warehouse and Associate Director at Hull Truck Theatre, where he was a key member of the team who planned and delivered the theatre's programme as part of Hull 2017 UK City of Culture. Tom's work as a director includes *Little Manfred* (Polka Theatre, Soldiers Arts Academy); *Freedom – March on Selma* (Yard Theatre); *Our Mutual Friend* (Hull Truck Theatre); *Defiance* (Hull Truck Theatre), *Who Cares* (JAM); *Face Me* (Pilot Theatre); *Beulah* (Flanagan Collective) and *Christmas Carol* (Arts Theatre). His work as an Associate Director includes *Under Milk Wood* (National Theatre) and *Sweat* (Donmar Warehouse and West End). Tom regularly directs and teaches at some of the UK's top drama-training institutions including RWCMD, Arts Ed,

RCSSD and Leeds Conservatoire. He was shortlisted for the RTST Peter Hall Directors Award and was an MGC Futures Bursary recipient.

Jim Harbourne
Composer and Sound Designer

Jim is an Edinburgh-based composer and sound designer. Career highlights include: *Feral* (Tortoise in a Nutshell, Cumbernauld Theatre); as part of *Brits off Broadway* at 59e59 Theatres New York, *Feral* was a *New York Times* Critics Pick, and was nominated for two Drama Desk Awards: 'Outstanding Music in a Play' and 'Unique Theatrical Experience'. *Feral* was also winner of a Fringe First Award, 2013, and has toured to Mexico, Denmark, Austria, Poland, Montenegro and extensively around the UK. *The Myth of the Singular Moment* (Jim Harbourne, Tortoise in a Nutshell) was Jim's debut play as a writer, performed at Summerhall, Edinburgh Festival Fringe 2018. Winner of Summerhall VAULT Award. Nominated for Scottish Arts Club 'Flying Artichoke' award. *Velvet Evening Seance* (written by Suzie Miller, directed by Ross MacKay) performed at Assembly Hall through Edinburgh Fringe 2017 and toured Scotland in Spring 2018. *Dette Er Vand* (Anna Bro, Teater Katapult) was Jim's first freelance international work, produced in Aarhus, Denmark in 2018.

Alice Hallifax
Set & Costume Designer

Alice is a designer working across theatre, live music, exhibition and installation, who has worked on productions in the UK, Romania, Spain and Mexico.

Recent projects include: *The Tempest* (Flute Theatre, Teatrul National Main Sorescu); *Pericles* (Flute Theatre, UK touring production); Donmar Warehouse LOCAL Residency (Donmar, Holborn Community Assoication); *The Noël Coward Room* (permanent exhibition at the Noel Coward Archive); *The Noël Coward Room: Art & Style* (an exhibition at the Guildhall Art Gallery); *And Still They Matter* (a live music performance at Coal Drops Yard); *The Border* (Theatre Centre/UK tour).

Recent design associate projects: *The Sun, The Moon, And the Stars*, *Extinct* and *After the End* with Peter McKintosh at Theatre Royal Stratford East.

As design support and model maker, Alice frequently works with Es Devlin and has previously worked with Lizzie Clachan, Rosie Elnile, Anna Fleischle, Michael Levine, Peter McKintosh, Joanna Scotcher and Tom Scutt. Alice has run theatre workshops with Donmar Warehouse, Theatre Centre and Artsdepot as well as previously working as a scenic painter, prop maker and mould maker for large scale productions including *Dreamgirls*, *The Ferryman* and *Harry Potter and the Cursed Child*.

Joseph Ed Thomas
Lighting Designer

Joseph has designed shows in London and throughout the UK. Highlights include: *Dr Zhivago*, *Annie Get Your Gun*, *Once* (London Palladium); *Collabro, Farewell Tour* (Adelphi Theatre and UK tour); *The Secret Garden*, *Camelot* (London Palladium); *John Owen Jones – Music of the Night Tour*, *Lucie Jones at Christmas* (Her Majesty's Theatre, St Davids Hall Cardiff); *Collabro, Greatest Hits Tour* (UK tour); *Under the Black Rock* (Arcola Theatre); *Cracked* (The Vaults); *Tango After Dark* (Co-design with Charlie Morgan Jones, Peacock Theatre, Sadler's Wells); *Little Voice* (UK tour).

As Associate Lighting Designer for Nic Farman: *John Owen Jones Celebrating his 50th Birthday – Live at Cadogan Hall*, *Lucie Jones and David Hunter LIVE!* (Cadogan Hall); *Rock Choir* (Birmingham REP); *Collabro, Christmas is Here* (Cadogan Hall) among others.

Sarah Penney
Producer

Sarah is a Hull-based producer from South Wales and a graduate of the University of Hull Drama and Theatre programme. She is part of fierce, feminist, fun theatre company The Roaring Girls, Senior Producer for Middle Child Theatre, Engagement Producer for Silent Uproar Productions, Producer of Absolutely Cultured and chair of the board of trustees for performing arts charity Concrete Youth. A multidisciplinary producer, Sarah has worked on large-scale outdoor projects, studio to mid-scale theatre productions, visual arts exhibitions, workshops and more. Highlights include *Luminarium* for Absolutely Cultured, *Advocacy in Action* for Regional Theatre Young Director Scheme, *PRSF New Music Biennial* for Southbank Centre, *I'm a Sexy Cat Woman Performing the Miracle of Life* for Lily Williams, *we used to be closer than this* for Middle Child Theatre, *Baize Moi* for Gareth Chambers and *Regional Young Actor's Ensemble* for Hull Truck Theatre.

Sarah Goodyear
Stage Manager

Sarah trained in Production Arts (Stage Management, Lighting and Sound) at Liverpool Community College. Credits include: *Aladdin*, *Robin Hood and the Babes in the Wood* (Oldham Coliseum Theatre); *Invisible Cities* (Manchester International Festival and Brisbane Festival); *Twelfth Night* (Octagon Theatre, Bolton); *Pomona* (Royal Exchange Theatre); *The Tale of Mr Tumble* (Opera House, Manchester); *The Last Testament of Lillian Bilocca* (Hull City of Culture); *Cat on a Hot Tin Roof* (Northern Stage and Royal & Derngate); *Mother Courage and Her Children* (Headlong, Royal Exchange Theatre); *There Has Possibly Been an Incident* (Soho Theatre); *Too Clever by Half* (Told by an Idiot, Royal Exchange Theatre) and *The Last Days of Troy* (Shakespeare's Globe Theatre).

Andy Ross
Set Builder

Andy is a performer and theatre-maker. Having trained as a theatre-maker in Hull, Andy furthered their clown training at The School of Lecoq, Phillippe Gauiler School and with Firenza Guidi (Artistic Director, NOFIT State Circus). Andy has focused training in clowning, puppetry and facilitating workshops in low-arts-engagement communities.

A new company dedicated to developing contemporary Northern stories and the writers behind them.

Terrain's aim is to collaborate with theatres nationally to increase capacity for Northern writers to get their plays into production and through this, enable the region's audiences to see more productions telling contemporary, diverse Yorkshire stories on our stages across the UK.

Terrain was set up in 2023 by director Tom Bellerby and producer Sarah Penney who are delighted to be debuting *Helen* as their first production with Theatre503.

Terrain Team

Cofounder and Director: Tom Bellerby

Cofounder and Producer: Sarah Penney

THEATRE 503

Theatre503 is at the forefront of identifying and nurturing new voices at the very start of their careers and launching them into the industry. They stage more early career playwrights than any other theatre in the world – with over 120 writers premiered each year from festivals of short pieces to full length productions, resulting in employment for over 1,000 freelance artists through their year-round programme.

Theatre503 provides a diverse pipeline of talent resulting in modern classics like *The Mountaintop* by Katori Hall and *Rotterdam* by Jon Brittain – both Olivier Award winners – to future classics like Yasmin Joseph's *J'Ouvert*, winner of the 2020 James Tait Black Prize which transferred to the West End/BBC Arts and *Wolfie* by Ross Willis, winner of the 2020 Writers Guild Award for Best New Play. Writers who began their creative life at Theatre503 are now writing for the likes of *The Crown*, *Succession*, *Doctor Who*, *Killing Eve* and *Normal People* and every single major subsidised theatre in the country now boasts a new play by a writer who started at Theatre503.

Theatre5O3 Team

Artistic Director	Lisa Spirling
Interim Executive Director	Jules Oakshett
Literary Manager	Steve Harper
Producer	Ceri Lothian
General Manager	Tash Berg
Carne Associate Director	Jade Lewis
Literary Associate	Lauretta Barrow
Trainee Assistant Producers	Tsipora St. Clair Knights
Technical Manager	Misha Mah
Marketing Officer	Millie Whittam
Administrator	Lizzie Akita
Development Coordinator	Heloise Gillingham

Theatre503's work would not be possible without the support of the following individuals, trusts and organisations:

We are particularly grateful to Philip and Christine Carne and the long-term support of The Carne Trust for our International Playwriting Award, the 503 Five and Carne Associate.

503Patrons: Ayla & Jon Hill, Berlin Associates, Caroline & Tim Langton, Cas & Philip Donald, Catharine Roos, Céline Gagnon, David Baxter & Carol Rahn, DavidsonMorris Solicitors, Eilene Davidson, Eric Bensaude, Erica Whyman, Freddie Hutchins & Oliver Rawlins, Gaskell & Jennifer Jacobs, Geraldine Sharpe-Newton, Ian Mill KC, Jack Tilbury/Plann, Laura Riddeck, Lisa Swinney, Lou Wilks & Tom Gowans, Louise Rawlins, Marcus Markou, Marianne Badrichani, Matthew Marren, Nick Hern Books, Pam Alexander & Roger Booker, Robert O'Dowd, Sally O'Neill, Sean Winnett, Steve Winter, The Bell Family, The Bloor Family, United Agents and all our 503Friends and Share the Drama supporters.

503Slate Supporters: Cas & Philip Donald, Concord Theatricals, Eilene Davidson, Gordon Bloor, Jean Doumanian, Kater Gordon, Kofi Owusu Bempah, Royce Bell.

Arts Council England Grants for the Arts, Backstage Trust, Battersea Power Station Foundation (Right to Write), Cockayne Grants for the Arts (503 Productions), Concord Theatricals (503 Playwriting Award), Garrick Charitable Trust, Noel Coward Foundation (Rapid Write Response), Theatres Trust, The Foyle Foundation, The Orseis Trust (503Five), Wandsworth Borough Council, Wimbledon Foundation (Five-O-Fresh).

HELEN

Maureen Lennon

For both my mums, Kathleen and Bridget.
And for Mally, forever on those Scottish Islands.

Characters

HELEN, *a woman*
BECCA, *her daughter*
EVIE, *Becca's daughter* (*should be played by the same actor as Helen*)

A Note on the Dialogue

A dash (–) at the end of a line indicates a thought that is broken.

A dash (–) on its own indicates a beat or breath in the scene.

A foward slash (/) indicates that lines are delivered in quick succession, often spoken over each other.

An ellipsis (…) indicates a trailing-off of the sentence.

This text went to press before the end of rehearsals and so may differ slightly from the play as performed.

1. The Beginning

BECCA. Mum /

HELEN. What?

BECCA. Mum, I think?

HELEN. What? What's going on?

BECCA. Mum, I think he's gone.

HELEN. What?

BECCA. I think he's dead, Mum. I think like this time he's actually gone.

HELEN. I, shit, I, has he not?

BECCA. No. Not for ages.

HELEN. He looks /

BECCA. Yeah.

HELEN. Last time, when he took that breath after ages though /

BECCA. No, he, I've been watching and he hasn't. I think I saw it, I think he sort of, went.

HELEN. Shit, shit I, just for a second I /

BECCA. It's okay.

HELEN. I can't believe I wasn't, you, you watching and me asleep. It wasn't long, was it /

BECCA. No. Only a little bit.

HELEN. You should have /

BECCA. I didn't know, I didn't realise.

HELEN. No.

–

–

HELEN. Should we?

BECCA. What?

HELEN. I mean, should we, I don't know, touch him, check? Check in?

BECCA. Check in?

HELEN. Oh, I don't know.

–

BECCA. Suddenly, suddenly it feels like /

HELEN. Yeah /

BECCA. His body it's, suddenly it's not /

HELEN. No.

BECCA. You could just take his hand maybe?

HELEN. Yeah I could. I should, to say bye, maybe.

BECCA. Okay.

HELEN. I just, I just don't want to.

BECCA. Okay.

HELEN. Suddenly he looks /

BECCA. Yeah.

HELEN. He's really gone, isn't he, he's really really /

BECCA. Dead.

HELEN. Yes. All of a sudden really very dead.

–

–

–

Should we, I don't know should we call someone?

BECCA. Maybe.

HELEN. I'm not that clear on the, what next, on the protocol
I suppose.

BECCA. No.

HELEN. Sorry I should know I just /

BECCA. It's okay.

–

–

HELEN. I didn't think it would feel like this.

BECCA. No.

HELEN. It feels like someone should be here.

BECCA. We're here.

HELEN. Yes.

BECCA. If we wait for long enough someone will come.

HELEN. That's true.

BECCA. That's one thing we're good at in here, isn't it?
Waiting.

–

HELEN. Oh Becca.

BECCA. Mum /

HELEN. I hope he knew we loved him.

BECCA. He did, Mum, he did.

HELEN. Come here.

–

–

At least it's over.

BECCA. Yeah.

HELEN. Is that terrible to say? But at least it's over, isn't it? At least we can get out of here, all these weeks of just /

BECCA. Waiting.

HELEN. Yes. At least it's the end.

BECCA. Yeah.

HELEN. Of this bit. Of this bit anyway.

2.

HELEN. Well that was /

BECCA. Yeah. Get these shoes off me.

HELEN. I told you /

BECCA. Okay /

HELEN. I told you they wouldn't be comfy /

BECCA. Yeah okay. Okay.

HELEN. I'm just saying /

BECCA. O. K.

HELEN. God I'm just so /

BECCA. Tired.

HELEN. Knackered.

BECCA. Yeah.

HELEN. I love you.

BECCA. I love you too.

HELEN. Do you want another drink?

BECCA. Do you need one?

HELEN. Becca /

BECCA. Just asking.

HELEN. Well don't.

BECCA. Okay.

HELEN. I'm going to have one.

BECCA. Okay. Do you think we should have stayed longer?

HELEN. Maybe.

BECCA. I'm not really sure, everyone there it seemed rude /

HELEN. I couldn't have another person tell me they were sorry, love.

BECCA. No.

HELEN. Or *such a character, he'll be missed, such happy years together* /

BECCA. Yeah /

HELEN. I just kept thinking it's like no one knew him, no one can think of anything to say except '*remember when he sent the wrong email to blah blah and it went all round the office*', what a great story, Dennis. What a great story about fuck-all.

BECCA. People are just being nice, Mum.

HELEN. I know.

BECCA. They're just trying to make us feel better.

HELEN. I know.

BECCA. It was nice to have him talked about.

HELEN. Yeah. Yeah I know.

–

–

    Your speech was lovely.

BECCA. Mum /

HELEN. No honestly it was, the things you said, and holding it together and everything, I'm proud of you, I'm really fucking proud of you.

BECCA. Okay.

HELEN. I couldn't remember where half those photos were taken /

BECCA. No?

HELEN. No. We looked, really happy.

BECCA. You were, we were happy /

HELEN. Were we?

BECCA. I just mean, yeah, yeah you were, weren't you?

HELEN. I suppose so. I suppose so just didn't –

I mean course we were, with you, darling, course you know we were just, I didn't expect it so soon, that's all. It made it seem so final, all our lives, those decisions all irreversible, immortalised in a slideshow to a Coldplay track /

BECCA. Mum /

HELEN. You know what I mean. Seems like last minute I was snogging him in The Crown, and wondering if I should have picked his mate instead /

BECCA. Mum /

HELEN. Well, he was better looking.

BECCA. Mum /

HELEN. It's been a long day.

BECCA. Yeah.

–

I was really nervous about it, today, like I was really nervous you know /

HELEN. Course you were /

BECCA. No, well I mean yeah that /

HELEN. You spoke really well /

BECCA. Yeah that but also /

HELEN. You've been really brave /

BECCA. Yeah the thing is, I was most nervous about what I was wearing.

HELEN. What?

BECCA. About this dress, about what to wear.

HELEN. You look gorgeous.

BECCA. That's what I mean, I was really nervous I wanted to look the part you know, I wanted people to see me and be like her dad just died, she looks amazing /

HELEN. Becca /

BECCA. And I've just been thinking about that all day, like that was what I was most nervous about.

HELEN. Becca, that's totally normal.

BECCA. Like what I was going to wear.

HELEN. It's not like we've got funeral outfits at the back of our cupboard.

BECCA. Does that make me a shit person?

HELEN. No. No, love /

BECCA. My dad's just died and I'm worrying about that. Does that make me / a

HELEN. It just makes you a person.

BECCA. Like I was performing, like I was performing this person of this girl whose dad just died /

HELEN. Your dad has just died /

BECCA. I know. I know that.

HELEN. It's gunna feel weird, love, it's gunna feel really strange there's no getting round that.

BECCA. It doesn't stop, does it, that's what you can't say to everyone there. It doesn't stop when you get through the front door.

HELEN. Yeah.

BECCA. Yeah.

–

HELEN. You do look gorgeous too.

BECCA. Oh fuck off.

HELEN. You do.

–

BECCA. Do you not wish you would've said something?

HELEN. No.

BECCA. You could've, I know you could've.

HELEN. I couldn't, darling. I –

I'm so proud of you that you could. I'm so –

but I just –

I couldn't get up there and say what, say he would've wanted this to be a celebration, cos would he, Becca, would he?

BECCA. Knowing Dad he probably would have wanted wailing at every opportunity.

HELEN. And the way everyone talks about it '*So brave, wasn't he, such a fighter. Such a shame he lost the battle. Such a shame it just got too much. If only he could have just summoned the strength.*' Fuck off.

BECCA. Mum /

HELEN. He didn't lose anything though, did he, Becca, he just died.

BECCA. They don't mean he failed, Mum, they just / mean

HELEN. We lost something. *We're* the ones that lost something, aren't we?

BECCA. Yes.

HELEN. And now he has to be perfect, all of a sudden we have to talk about him like he's perfect.

If I could have got up there and said he was a cunt, no cos he was, wasn't he, a cunt who once parked the car across the road and stopped all the traffic until I said I was sorry cos we'd had a row, or left you on the street cos he'd kicked you out the car for a tantrum when you were six, or went home that first night I had you in the hospital cos he couldn't sleep in a chair even though I was sleeping with six stiches in my vagina /

BECCA. Mum /

HELEN. Or left dirty tissues on the floor under the bed, or left the washing up till morning, or hummed that tune over and over after he saw the last James Bond, do you remember? Till we were about ready to kill him. And that noise, that noise he used to make at the back of his throat, that disgusting noise that –

BECCA. Mum /

HELEN. No if I could've. If I could've got up there and said he was a cunt and I'm angry and he was ours and we love him and he's gone now, he's gone now, he's gone now, he's gone now, he's gone now, he's gone now and there is nothing to celebrate about that big fuck-off emptiness I'm having to –

My daughter is having to, when she shouldn't. If I could say all that I would've but –

–

BECCA. You could. You could and it would've been great.

HELEN. Yeah.

BECCA. Everyone would have cried.

HELEN. Yeah, yeah well maybe. Just didn't seem like the thing, did it.

–

–

–

Here you go.

BECCA. Thanks.

HELEN. Cheers.

BECCA. Cheers.

–

What shall we do now?

HELEN. Do you want to order a pizza?

3.

BECCA. Are you going to bed?

HELEN. Oh I'm just, yeah. Yeah in a bit maybe.

BECCA. Last night you stayed in the chair.

HELEN. Did I?

BECCA. Yeah cos I was waiting, to, I couldn't sleep actually and I was just lying /

HELEN. Yeah.

BECCA. And you didn't come up.

HELEN. No.

BECCA. So tonight /

HELEN. Maybe.

BECCA. It's quite lonely, up there, with you down here,
   I dunno, shouldn't make a difference but it's /

HELEN. Yeah.

   –

   I get that. I get that just, sometimes, sometimes I can't face it.

BECCA. Yeah.

HELEN. Sometimes, because I roll over, you know, and there's
   this space, suddenly, I've forgotten it will be there but it is /

BECCA. Yes /

HELEN. And I could just keep on rolling. I could just –

   All that space it's –

BECCA. Yeah.

HELEN. It will get easier I think, it will get less sharp anyway,
   won't it?

   –

BECCA. What if I, like when I was little what if I?

HELEN. That would be nice.

BECCA. I've got my own pillow.

HELEN. Alright. Don't cover-hog though /

BECCA. I don't /

HELEN. Excuse me /

BECCA. Don't snore then /

HELEN. I don't /

BECCA. Yeah right. Dunno how he put up with it. (*Snores*.)

HELEN. I'll kick you out.

BECCA. You won't.

HELEN. No. I won't.

4.

HELEN. You look /

BECCA. Yeah. You too.

HELEN. Got to make the effort.

BECCA. First day back.

HELEN. It's going to be fine.

BECCA. I hope so.

HELEN. Everyone knows, you know? I've spoken to your teachers /

BECCA. Yeah, Mum.

HELEN. If you need any time, just step out.

BECCA. I will.

HELEN. Everyone will understand.

BECCA. I know.

HELEN. Okay.

BECCA. You too.

HELEN. What?

BECCA. If it gets too much /

HELEN. Oh you've spoken to my boss, have you?

BECCA. I could if you want.

HELEN. Right.

BECCA. Send you with a note.

HELEN. Thanks.

BECCA. Yeah.

HELEN. Ready?

BECCA. Ready.

HELEN. You look the part.

BECCA. You too.

HELEN. Better get on with it then, eh? Don't want to be late.

BECCA. Yeah.

HELEN. I'll pick you up tonight?

BECCA. Won't you be at /

HELEN. Tonight I will.

BECCA. I don't mind getting the bus, now Dad isn't, I know it's
    not on your way home like it was for / him

HELEN. I'll do it.

BECCA. Okay.

HELEN. Just today.

BECCA. Okay.

HELEN. Okay. Okay. Let's go.

5.

BECCA. I've been waiting.

HELEN. Okay –

BECCA. No just I've been waiting for you quite a while
    actually.

HELEN. Right. Well I would've /

BECCA. Sorry?

HELEN. Well I would've been quiet, coming in /

BECCA. That's not the /

HELEN. I know you've got exams in the morning I / wouldn't

BECCA. That's not the point really /

HELEN. Isn't it?

BECCA. Not really.

HELEN. Okay.

–

BECCA. You stink.

HELEN. What?

BECCA. Of alcohol you stink.

HELEN. Right, well I don't know if that's any of / your

BECCA. One drink you said.

HELEN. What?

BECCA. One drink after work.

HELEN. Okay well I think we're forgetting who's the teenager / here

BECCA. You think?

HELEN. I'm finding you rude actually rude and /

BECCA. One drink after work it's 2 a.m. /

HELEN. Let's talk about this in the morning.

BECCA. Lipstick round your face /

HELEN. I really don't need this now, water /

BECCA. State of you, Mum, like what / are

HELEN. A glass of water and I'm going to / bed

BECCA. And that, in the car, like that's /

HELEN. What?

BECCA. In the car. What was that?

HELEN. What do you mean 'in the car'?

BECCA. Just now.

HELEN. Have you been watching me?

BECCA. Not exactly hard is it, half the neighbours could have /

HELEN. That's so totally inappropriate /

BECCA. I mean what do you think you're / doing

HELEN. That is so completely inappropriate I think you /
should

BECCA. Come down to get a drink find my mother getting
fingered in the street /

HELEN. That's ridiculous, don't exaggerate now /

BECCA. All over some, some random fucking bloke /

HELEN. I think you should go to bed, I think you should go to
bed now /

BECCA. Fucking free show for the neighbours, don't worry
about her she's lost her husband and now she thinks she's
a porn star /

HELEN. Stop it. Stop it right now alright.

BECCA. Give her a bottle of Pinot and she's anyone's /

HELEN. I mean it /

BECCA. Couldn't wait to move on, could she, barely fucking in
the ground and there she / is

HELEN. Don't you DARE okay. Don't you fucking DARE.
Not that. Not about your dad. Not like this means he doesn't
matter okay. Don't you dare, to me. Don't you –

–

BECCA. Okay. Okay.

–

HELEN. That's not fair, is it? You know it's not fair.

BECCA. Okay. Okay. I'm sorry.

–

HELEN. Me too. Fuck, me too.

BECCA. Mum?

HELEN. I think I'm going to be sick?

BECCA. Mum /

HELEN. Fuck, I think /

BECCA. Alright, alright get over the sink.

HELEN. I'm just /

BECCA. I've got you, I've got your hair just /

HELEN. Gross /

BECCA. Don't worry get it all up /

HELEN. God I'm sorry /

BECCA. No don't /

HELEN. I shouldn't be doing, I mean you're sixteen you're the one that should be /

BECCA. Yeah well I have, haven't I, just not in front of you.

HELEN. Have you? Why not in front of me?

BECCA. You're my mum.

HELEN. You can have a drink in front of me, you don't have to, I mean I'd rather that than you hide / it

BECCA. Mum.

HELEN. Yeah, yeah alright. I'm your mum. Oh shit.

BECCA. Keep going it'll be done in a minute.

HELEN. Yeah.

BECCA. Yeah.

–

–

Better?

HELEN. A bit. Thank you.

BECCA. Okay.

–

–

HELEN. He's not some random bloke.

BECCA. What?

HELEN. He's not some random bloke. I work with him.

BECCA. Alright.

HELEN. Known him for years actually. Me and your dad used
to go for meals with him and his wife.

BECCA. Well that's fucked up.

HELEN. He's always had a thing for me. We used to joke about
it. Hands like an octopus. We used to joke about it, all the
time.

BECCA. Okay.

HELEN. What a sleaze, what a pathetic gropey sweaty sleaze.
Fuck what's that make me, eh?

BECCA. Mum?

HELEN. I dunno, I'm sorry I just, I just, tonight I –

You know I love being your mum, right?

BECCA. Don't be silly.

HELEN. Yeah but you know I do, right?

BECCA. Yeah, Mum. Yeah I know.

HELEN. And that's, most of the time that's enough, isn't it,
that's –

But, but I just, sometimes –

What no one tells you, when your dad died, what no one tells you is all of a sudden that person who knew you as that thing, that's gone /

BECCA. What?

HELEN. Like twenty years we've been, and you don't want to hear this cos he's your dad but we were, you know, he was good at making me feel wanted, sexy, sex, sex you know /

BECCA. Stop saying sex, Mum.

HELEN. Alright, alight. Sorry I just mean suddenly he's gone and no one makes me feel /

BECCA. Yeah.

HELEN. Sometimes I'm just so angry. And I feel like, I feel like I've lost that thing, that thing inside me where I knew I was, I had it, we had it you know, whatever that was.

And tonight, he was just there, after work, just there with his hands, with his – making it clear I could if I wanted to, I –

And I did I just –

I'm sorry you saw –

BECCA. Me too.

HELEN. If it makes you feel better it was horrible. It was, it was like I wasn't even there, I was just watching him touch me with those hands, those dead hands /

BECCA. Mum /

HELEN. And I thought, god I wish your dad was here so we could laugh about this. Me getting snogged by gropey mcgroperson me just letting it –

BECCA. It's okay, Mum.

HELEN. God I wish he /

BECCA. Yeah. Me too.

HELEN. Yeah. State of me, eh.

BECCA. Of us.

HELEN. Yeah. State of us. Yeah.

6.

BECCA. Do we just? /

HELEN. Yeah, I mean I suppose, I suppose so.

BECCA. It doesn't seem like they're really going to go very far.

HELEN. Well maybe if you really chuck, get your arm right in.

BECCA. Okay.

HELEN. I mean I didn't know it would be this wet.

BECCA. Don't know why, it always is.

HELEN. I know but somehow in my head I thought it'd be different this time, you know, cold blue skies, a bit of a breeze that catches and carries them away, like he's a hawk.

BECCA. A hawk?

HELEN. Yeah. A bird of prey.

BECCA. You're a twat.

HELEN. Massive you know, elegant, imposing.

BECCA. Think a pigeon would be more like Dad.

HELEN. A pigeon? He was a handsome man your dad.

BECCA. Alright a crow then.

HELEN. A crow?!

BECCA. Yeah you know cos they do that noise a bit /

HELEN. Cawkkk cawwwkkk cawwwwk.

BECCA. Yeah. That. Sounds just like his /

HELEN. Laugh. Yeah. It does.

BECCA. I wish you'd brought gloves for this bit.

HELEN. What?

BECCA. I wish you'd brought gloves or something, cos this is just, I mean I didn't realise but in the wet they're sort of clumping together, aren't they /

HELEN. Yeah well I suppose it makes them sort of runny /

BECCA. And I hadn't really thought about it but now I'm holding them, actually holding them in my hand /

HELEN. Oh /

BECCA. And they're a sort of wet lumpy mess /

HELEN. Well maybe put them back in /

BECCA. And that's sort of gross, a wet lumpy mess of Dad, that's sort of /

HELEN. Well put them back in, here, put them, and we can sort of fling them out the top /

BECCA. I don't know if they'll fling now they're wet.

HELEN. Well let's have a go.

BECCA. Okay.

HELEN. Ready?

BECCA. Should we, I dunno should we sort of say something /

HELEN. Maybe /

BECCA. Just to make it a bit more /

HELEN. Yeah /

BECCA. Okay. Bye Dad.

HELEN. Bye.

BECCA. We love you.

HELEN. You loved it here, you always said to me.

BECCA. You always said you could live here.

HELEN. At the top of the stones, what are they called?

BECCA. A cairn /

HELEN. Yeah. The cairn. I remember you climbing up, right up to this top bit every time we got to the top of this hill and Becca would flop on the ground in a mood /

BECCA. I wouldn't /

HELEN. Because we'd made her use her legs. You'd always climb up to the top and take big gulps of air and beat your chest and make that noise /

BECCA. *Ahhhhoooooooohhhaaaaaaaaaaaaa!*

HELEN. Yeah that one right down the valley.

BECCA. Prat.

HELEN. '*Look at that, Helen, just look at it.*'

I don't know what you were looking at. You always said there was a view, under the cloud, when it wasn't raining, you always said if the weather was right you could see for miles.

BECCA. I've never been here when it wasn't raining.

HELEN. Me neither.

BECCA. '*I could live here.*'

HELEN. I hope you meant it.

BECCA. Me too.

HELEN. *Ahhhhhhhoohhhhhhhhhaaaaaaaaaaaaaaaaaaa.*

BECCA. Bye. We love you.

HELEN. We really really love you.

–

–

Well that /

BECCA. It sort of worked. Most of them went /

HELEN. Just those that are still up your arm /

BECCA. And there's a bit down your waterproof trouser /

HELEN. Yeah.

BECCA. Sorry, Dad. But mostly.

HELEN. We've tried.

BECCA. Yeah. Yeah we have.

    –

    –

    Do you feel?

HELEN. I feel wet, mostly.

BECCA. Yeah. I feel like, I feel like it's a nice place to leave
    him.

HELEN. Do you?

BECCA. Yeah. I think so, do you?

HELEN. I don't know.

BECCA. At least we can think of him here now. When it comes
    in our heads, all this space, at least, not like that hospital
    room, down all those stairs with that artificial light.

HELEN. Or in the bathroom cupboard.

BECCA. Or in the bathroom cupboard where you insisted he
    live these last few months.

HELEN. More hygienic.

BECCA. In that bloody bucket. At least now we can think of
    him out here. In this. In all this.

HELEN. Yeah. Yeah. We can try.

BECCA. *Ahhhhhooohhhhhhaaaaaa. I could live here.*

HELEN. We. Love. You.

7.

BECCA. I CAN'T BELIEVE YOU DID THAT

HELEN. What?

BECCA. Do you have to always, it's, everyone from school was there /

HELEN. I don't understand what's meant to be so terrible.

BECCA. You always do things like this, you always /

HELEN. What was so terrible, I was just proud, I was just /

BECCA. I asked you. I fucking. I said if you were going to come, could you make the effort, just for one evening, just for one fucking night not to be so embarrassing.

HELEN. I don't understand what I'm meant to have done.

BECCA. No one else's parents stood up.

HELEN. What?

BECCA. Standing up, in front of everyone, whooping, cheering /

HELEN. I was just proud /

BECCA. No one else's parents had to make a scene /

HELEN. I was just proud of you, all A-stars, your results. It's a big thing, GCSE's, it's huge /

BECCA. Tonight was a posh evening. Formal. I warned you /

HELEN. I think you're being extremely ungrateful /

BECCA. No one else's parents fell off their chair cos they'd had about twelve of the complimentary wines /

HELEN. That is completely unfair /

BECCA. I'm already the girl whose dad died now you have to go and be a complete mess too.

HELEN. I'm allowed to express the fact I'm proud of you.

BECCA. It's not that though, is it, it's you, making it about you, not being normal, being /

HELEN. I think you need to think about what you're saying /

BECCA. You're a mess. Do you ever think that? You're a mess.

HELEN. I'm warning you to stop /

BECCA. Dad wouldn't have done this, if he'd been the one that was still here he wouldn't have been like this.

HELEN. Well he's not and I am okay so just think about what you're / saying

BECCA. You're pathetic. Everyone thinks it. Hanging off Mr Malory's arm tonight on the way to the car, like he might / take

HELEN. Don't just make stuff up now.

BECCA. I just wanted, for one evening I just wanted you to hold it together.

HELEN. You know it might not have occurred to you but I don't live my life just to embarrass you, just to go places and get shouted at by my mean / daughter

BECCA. Sometimes, sometimes I wish it was you instead of Dad.

–

–

HELEN. Go to your room.

BECCA. Sometimes like tonight.

HELEN. Go to your room right now.

BECCA. It's not fair!

HELEN. I don't want to see you, I don't want to –

BECCA. Ahhhahahahaahahahah!

HELEN. GO TO YOUR ROOM. You ungrateful, you spiteful,
    you, you, oh god you, GO.

BECCA. I WISH IT WAS YOU.

    –

    –

HELEN. You don't mean that.

BECCA. I do.

HELEN. One day you're going to be really sorry you said that.

BECCA. I won't.

HELEN. You will. I hope you will.

8.

HELEN. Who'd have thought it would be this much stuff I hope
    it's all going to fit in your room /

BECCA. It will.

HELEN. They didn't look that big when we looked round, did
    they?

BECCA. It'll fit.

HELEN. And the kitchen was tiny.

BECCA. Well I probably won't spend that much time in there.

HELEN. You need to eat properly, Becca.

BECCA. Yeah yeah.

HELEN. I mean it.

BECCA. Okay.

HELEN. Do you think it's all going to fit in the car?

BECCA. Yes.

HELEN. You need to be able to see out the back window.

BECCA. It'll be fine.

HELEN. Yeah, yeah okay.

BECCA. Okay.

–

HELEN. Right, right well then. Better get you loaded up, hadn't
we. Don't want you getting there too late.

BECCA. No.

HELEN. University, it's, I'm really proud of you, your dad
would've been so –

God I'm going to miss you.

–

BECCA. I don't have to go.

HELEN. Don't be silly.

BECCA. I actually mean it, I actually mean I could stay, just cos
this is what people think you do, what people /

HELEN. I'm excited for you.

BECCA. I can come back a lot, I can come back most weekends
can't I?

HELEN. If you want to /

BECCA. I might even come back next weekend.

HELEN. Becca /

BECCA. What?

HELEN. It's going to be fine. You don't have to worry about
me.

BECCA. Okay.

HELEN. It's time you stopped worrying and was a proper
teenager /

BECCA. Right.

HELEN. I'm going to miss you but I'm going to be fine.

BECCA. Okay.

–

What if I'm not?

HELEN. What?

BECCA. Fine.

HELEN. What?

BECCA. The thing is, like, I'm not sure, I'm not sure actually that I want to go.

HELEN. What?

BECCA. The more I think about it, I'm not sure I want to.

HELEN. It's normal to be nervous, it's totally normal. I get it. All new start, it's hard. But, it's also kind of brilliant. You can be whoever you want. You can get really into piercings or gin or like dungarees or something. I'm almost jealous.

BECCA. I'm not normal nervous, I'm just, I don't want / to

HELEN. If this is about me, I really am going to be fine.

BECCA. It's not about you.

HELEN. I've got plans work, friends, I /

BECCA. It's not about you.

HELEN. Okay.

–

Is it about Dad?

–

He would have loved to be here, you know. He would have loved to get your room sorted, and settled, and unpack all your boxes.

BECCA. I know.

HELEN. I know that makes it sad, I know that's –

But you're gunna meet people, and learn stuff, and some of it will be sad but also it will be new.

BECCA. I don't want new. I don't want new people, I don't want to, to have to explain, to have to –

Cos I'm not, I'm not fun any more.

HELEN. What? Don't be stupid.

BECCA. No, I'm not. Honestly. I can't be because there is this feeling pressing down on my chest all the time. Even when I'm pretending all the time it's like someone is pressing hard there /

HELEN. I know, love /

BECCA. No because there is. And that means, I'm not –

HELEN. People will understand, your friends here have been so good.

BECCA. Yeah, yeah cos they know me but new people /

HELEN. Will be nice. You can explain.

BECCA. Explain how? Like, do I just say my dad's dead when I'm introducing myself? Fresher's night out, 'Hi nice to meet you, I'm Becca, my dad's dead.'

HELEN. Well no maybe not then no /

BECCA. When though? Cos it's quite a big thing, isn't it, it's quite a big thing to be wondering about, or getting asked about.

HELEN. Yeah.

BECCA. And then they'll say 'When?' and I'll say, 'Three years ago' and they'll say, 'Oh, oh sorry' but as if they mean that's a long time haven't you got over it yet? /

HELEN. Three years is not a long time, love, no one expects /

BECCA. And I'll say I'll say no, no I haven't cos there's this thing pressing on my chest here, and it won't, it might not ever –

HELEN. You are doing so brilliantly. No one expects /

BECCA. The thing is three years feels like forever from the outside, I can tell, I can tell even with people now.

HELEN. Come here. Listen to me.

You tell people when you want to okay, you be as sad or happy as you want to be. Because even when you're pretending you are more funny and brilliant than most people in the room /

BECCA. Mum, that's not /

HELEN. And some people might not get it but fuck 'em.

BECCA. Mum.

HELEN. No honestly. Fuck them. And I'm always here and I'm always on the phone. But you can do this, I know you can.

BECCA. Okay.

–

HELEN. Are you sure you don't want me to drive?

BECCA. You can't fit in the car.

HELEN. No. No I suppose not.

9.

HELEN. It's good to see you /

BECCA. Right.

HELEN. I've missed you.

BECCA. Yeah, me too.

HELEN. You look, god you look /

BECCA. Don't, Mum.

HELEN. No. I've brought your stuff, some things they said you can have /

BECCA. Right.

HELEN. PJs, new pants, just in case you have to stay over night.

BECCA. Okay.

–

HELEN. God Becca you look /

BECCA. Mum, don't.

HELEN. No, no just I can't. I can't believe you –

BECCA. I'm sorry I haven't been home.

HELEN. It's okay, it's okay.

BECCA. Everything just got a bit, everything just got a bit hard.

HELEN. Well you're coming home with me now, okay, you're coming home with me now and we're going to get you all the help you need and when you're ready you can come back and do it on your own terms /

BECCA. I've got exams /

HELEN. It doesn't matter.

BECCA. I think if I just /

HELEN. You can do this year again.

BECCA. I don't want to fail, Mum.

HELEN. You can defer, it's not failing.

BECCA. I think it's really important I /

HELEN. No. You're coming home with me. It's really important I look after you. It's really important you're okay.

BECCA. Okay. Okay thanks. Thank you.

–

HELEN. These might be –

Yes well I suppose pyjamas are meant to be big, comfy. God you look /

BECCA. Please don't, Mum /

HELEN. If someone hadn't have found you /

BECCA. I don't think it was that big a deal.

HELEN. They said your heart rate was so low, so thin that your heart could've –

That's why you collapsed. They say your heart, Becca, your heart /

BECCA. Mum /

HELEN. I don't understand you've never, I mean you've always been gorgeous, you've always been absolutely gorgeous you don't need to worry, you don' need to do this to your /

BECCA. I'm not sure it's really about that / for me

HELEN. No one needs to do this to themselves /

BECCA. You're not listening you don't get it all. You don't /

HELEN. Well I just /

BECCA. You never listen.

HELEN. I just don't get / why

BECCA. I knew you'd be like this. I knew it.

HELEN. I, I'm –

I'm sorry. I'm sorry. Maybe you could help me understand.

–

BECCA. I just, I just needed to feel… To be able to make things stop for a bit, so I couldn't, so I couldn't feel, things. Feel me.

I could be in control. The routine, and the, numbness, and, and, I don't know how to explain. I just, it made things better. For a bit. It made it feel like I had it all sorted out.

–

HELEN. I can understand that. I can understand wanting to feel like that.

BECCA. Yes.

HELEN. None of us have got it all sorted out though, love. None of us have.

BECCA. I know.

HELEN. Somehow we need to learn how to make that okay.

BECCA. How?

HELEN. I don't know. But we'll figure it out. We'll figure it out okay?

10.

HELEN. I'm so proud of you.

BECCA. Thank you.

HELEN. You've done it.

BECCA. Four years /

HELEN. Alright few hiccups but you've done it.

BECCA. Thanks.

HELEN. A gown suits you.

BECCA. It's the shape.

HELEN. It's the gravitas.

BECCA. Right.

HELEN. To you. To you and your new future.

BECCA. Whatever that might be.

HELEN. Whatever.

BECCA. Can't wait to fail to get a job.

HELEN. You'll do just fine.

BECCA. Thanks.

HELEN. You will, you always do.

BECCA. Do you think we should really have another?

HELEN. We're celebrating.

BECCA. Mum /

HELEN. I promise not to whoop in the ceremony I remember you don't like that /

BECCA. Mum /

HELEN. We're fine I can still stand on one leg and touch my nose.

BECCA. Remember we're meeting Dave after so...

HELEN. Of course. I remember, I'm very excited. The famous Dave.

BECCA. Just make sure you're not too –

HELEN. Too?

BECCA. You know.

HELEN. I didn't realise people were still called Dave. Unless they were born at forty with a plumbing kit in their hand.

BECCA. Too much like that.

HELEN. I won't. And he's graduating today too?

BECCA. Yesterday. He's in a different school.

HELEN. Which is?

BECCA. Business. Business and marketing.

HELEN. Really?

BECCA. Mum.

HELEN. Well, that seems very, *entrepreneurial*.

BECCA. He got a first.

HELEN. Amazing, I'm sure he'll turn it into excellent capital.

BECCA. Try and be nice.

HELEN. I'll be very charming.

BECCA. Not too charming.

HELEN. What's that meant to mean?

BECCA. You know exactly what it means.

HELEN. Come here. I'm so proud of you.

BECCA. I know.

HELEN. You really like this one?

BECCA. Yes.

HELEN. And he likes you?

BECCA. Yes.

HELEN. Well at least I know he's not stupid then.

BECCA. Mum!

HELEN. I can't wait.

11.

HELEN. It's fine /

No don't worry I know /

Yeah, I know, I know you're sorry.

I'll be fine.

First Christmas together is important. We can do ours another day.

Exactly, just me and you, isn't it, we can do it whenever.

No don't worry, I'll be fine, I mean it. I'm sure you'll have much more fun there anyway, no one crying over the pudding like last year.

No, no I was joking, that was a joke, I am going to be fine honestly.

It's nice that he's got such a big family, it's really nice and I'm so pleased they're close. That's important.

Yeah maybe. I might go there, or to Aunty Sal's if I want to, I'm sure there's lots of places I can go if I decide I don't want to be on my own.

Please don't feel guilty. No honestly. No it's fine honestly I'll see you after, when you come home.

You'll, be fine, you'll eat, you've been eating, haven't you?

Sorry, sorry I had to ask. I know. I know you will. Yes okay.

Yes you can pop back before I'm back at work, for a few days, we'll do something then.

I'll keep the tree up.

No I want you to have a nice time, I really do.

Yes.

Love you too. Love you.

It really is fine.

12.

BECCA. You could have said.

HELEN. I'm saying now.

BECCA. I think it's a mistake.

HELEN. I've put all your boxes in the kitchen, if you could decide what needs to come with me and what needs to /

BECCA. We've always lived here /

HELEN. Yes, love, but /

BECCA. I mean this is a pretty big deal, to just come home and find it's all /

HELEN. It's too big, it's too big for just me.

BECCA. It's not just you though, is it?

HELEN. Most of the time it is. Especially with your internship now /

BECCA. I still come home some weekends /

HELEN. When you're not at David's.

BECCA. Mum /

HELEN. There's a spare room at the new place, your room, you can decorate it.

BECCA. A flat? I haven't even seen it. You don't want a flat, / do you

HELEN. It's nice, it's new, all clean lines and straight walls /

BECCA. I haven't even, I mean I could have got to look at it /

HELEN. We had to move fast, it's a new build and it's a good investment, the estate agent said they're being snapped up.

BECCA. I bet he did.

HELEN. We could go and look at it later if you want? Get a feel.

BECCA. This is our home.

HELEN. Yes but /

BECCA. It's our, I was born here /

HELEN. Well you were born in hospital actually but I take your point.

BECCA. Where are you going to put everything in a flat?

HELEN. I'm going to get rid of it mostly, new start.

BECCA. Dad's stuff?

HELEN. Well it's still. Some of it's in boxes and some of it's still hung up and I was hoping you could help me, this weekend, sort through what we want to keep and what we want to –

BECCA. Mum /

HELEN. I know, I know but sometime we have to, sometime we /

BECCA. Dad, like just out on the rubbish pile /

HELEN. DON'T.

BECCA. Well that's what it is though, isn't it?

HELEN. It's not him, Becca. He's not old shirts that I've left in the wardrobe, is he? I can't just. Just me rattling round this big house. Coming round a corner half-expecting your dad –

And you when you were little –

Half-expecting all three of us to –

BECCA. I like that. I like coming back and finding all that.

HELEN. Yes because you come back to find it but then *you* get to leave.

BECCA. Mum /

HELEN. Here. I can't, I –

The coffee cups are still in the same place, cos that's where the coffee cups live, right? But something, I need something to be different.

BECCA. We're not suddenly going to stop missing him in
a new flat with laminate floors.

HELEN. I don't think that, I'm not stupid. But I'm just saying
I need, I need *this*, Becca. Fresh start.

BECCA. Okay.

HELEN. You have to let me do that.

BECCA. Okay. Okay. I get it, I will.

HELEN. Thank you.

BECCA. It's okay.

HELEN. And it hasn't got laminate floors.

BECCA. What?

HELEN. The flat. It's got wood floors, Oak actually.

BECCA. Oh, well that's lovely.

HELEN. Yes. Yes it is.

13.

BECCA. Fuck /

HELEN. It's fine.

BECCA. Fuck I'm nervous.

HELEN. You're going to be fine. Have a drink.

BECCA. I'm really really fucking nervous.

HELEN. You'll be fine when you're up there. You look perfect.

BECCA. Were you nervous?

HELEN. What?

BECCA. When you married Dad, were you nervous?

HELEN. I was furious.

BECCA. What?

HELEN. I was furious.

BECCA. I don't understand.

HELEN. I was furious, because I had to pull his head out the bog to get him there. He couldn't stop being sick.

BECCA. Was he ill?

HELEN. Ill. He was fucking hungover. He'd been out until god knows when on his stag do, he was green and I'd been told by a fair few of his friends he'd spent the last part of the evening snogging the barmaid /

BECCA. Fuck /

HELEN. Yeah exactly.

BECCA. But you were still, I mean you still did it.

HELEN. We had a church full of people, our parents, we'd spent our only few quid of savings on the buffet /

BECCA. But, but I mean, that wasn't Dad, he must've just been drunk /

HELEN. Yeah, yeah maybe, that's what he always said.

BECCA. Always?

HELEN. It wasn't the only time.

BECCA. You're not making me feel much better.

HELEN. Sorry, just saying it could be worse than nerves, you could have doubts too.

BECCA. You had doubts?

HELEN. Wouldn't you?

BECCA. I'm not sure now is the right time to be telling me this.

HELEN. Look, I'm just trying to say it doesn't have to be perfect, it's the next bit that matters.

BECCA. I always thought that, you and Dad, I always thought you were the perfect, partners you know, meant to be /

HELEN. I don't know if anyone's meant to be, Becca /

BECCA. Great, glad you're revealing this philosophy now.

HELEN. No, I mean, I mean we were, partners, but we, we made that happen. We never just knew, there were decisions all along the way we could have done differently, we could have ended up with other people, it's, but you stick with the decisions you've made, right, you stick with each other, that's what makes it.

BECCA. Do you ever wish it wasn't, I mean now do you ever wish you hadn't though, with Dad, do you ever wish /

HELEN. When you love someone and you build a life, that's what matters, that's what –

Cos you will probably betray each other, and hurt each other, and annoy each other but also you will share in so much you will, the stuff you build together just by being there –

And you, our family, I never wished I could change your dad, my husband maybe sometimes but, your dad –

I just wish we'd had a bit more of it, you know –

BECCA. Yeah.

HELEN. I wish he could see you today.

BECCA. Me too.

HELEN. You look, god you look –

You're going to be so happy.

BECCA. I hope so.

HELEN. I know so. I wish he was here to walk you /

BECCA. Yes. Yes me too but also, I'm so glad it's you, Mum.

HELEN. God I'm, we're both crying again, aren't we /

BECCA. Our make-up /

HELEN. I know, I know pull it together.

Come on. Come on then, we better get you in there and get on with it.

14.

BECCA. You can't keep doing this?

HELEN. What?

BECCA. This. This, you yesterday you can't keep doing it.

HELEN. I don't know what / you

BECCA. You don't even remember, do you?

HELEN. Do I have to be attacked, first thing in a morning?
I didn't even know you were coming back this weekend.

BECCA. I'm back because I got a phone call at work from your boss.

HELEN. Oh.

BECCA. Can you remember why that might be?

HELEN. I think I'd prefer to talk about this another time.

BECCA. I'm sure you would.

HELEN. I haven't asked you to just come in and lecture /

BECCA. He wanted me to come and pick you up, apparently, you'd come into work in a state so bad they didn't even feel comfortable sending you home alone.

HELEN. It's ridiculous, I'd only had a couple /

BECCA. You couldn't stand up, Mum.

HELEN. I'm a grown woman I don't need to be told what to /

BECCA. On a Friday at work. Coming back from lunch obviously hammered /

HELEN. It's none of your business /

BECCA. And this isn't the first time, is it? This isn't the first time they've noticed, though it might be the worst.

HELEN. I'd appreciate it if you'd all keep your / nose

BECCA. What did you think was going to happen? Honestly when you decided that was okay what did you think was going to / happen

HELEN. This is just a total misrepresentation.

BECCA. You can't keep trying to twist things it's gone too far this time.

HELEN. I haven't asked for your opinion, for you to get involved.

BECCA. I am involved though, aren't I? I am involved because I can't not be.

HELEN. It's none of your business.

BECCA. Who else is going to look after you /

HELEN. I don't need / looking after

BECCA. We need to talk about this, to sort it out, it's gone too far.

HELEN. I'm not a child I don't need looking after.

BECCA. You do.

HELEN. I'd like you to leave now.

BECCA. We need to talk about this, properly.

HELEN. I'd like you to leave my house. I'll ring you when we've both calmed down.

BECCA. I really need you to listen to me, I really need you to get help.

HELEN. Now please.

BECCA. Mum /

HELEN. I'm fine I don't need help.

BECCA. Mum.

HELEN. Go home.

BECCA. YOU CAN'T KEEP DOING THIS I CAN'T KEEP DOING THIS WITH YOU.

–

HELEN. I, I'm, I.

–

BECCA. I'm sorry I can't I don't have the energy.

HELEN. I didn't ask you to come.

BECCA. No but other people did, because they don't know how to make it better either.

HELEN. This week /

BECCA. Yes, this week, this month they're difficult. Do you think I don't recognise that? Do you think that's not true for me too /

HELEN. Of course it is.

BECCA. I understand, alright. But you can't /

HELEN. I just keep seeing him in the hospital, every year, this week, this weather, those last few hours of waiting, his, his, you know his –

BECCA. I know /

HELEN. I just –

BECCA. This week isn't the problem, is it though, Mum? If it was just this week it wouldn't be a problem.

HELEN. I don't have a problem.

BECCA. No? I do, I do because my dad is gone, and you, you are –

And it is getting worse and I don't know how to help you.

HELEN. Sometimes I feel so lonely.

BECCA. I know.

HELEN. I lost my husband.

BECCA. I know. I know but that isn't the problem right now, is it?

–

When I, at Uni when I went into hospital you said to me, it's okay not to control it, it's okay to be lonely, just feel it, none of us have it figured out.

HELEN. Yes.

BECCA. We're going to get you help. We're going to get you through this, you said.

HELEN. Yes.

BECCA. And we did, sort of, so I could live with it, we did.

HELEN. Yes.

BECCA. Mum, I want to get you through this.

HELEN. I'm, I'm not /

BECCA. I want to get you help. Tell me you've got a problem so we can. First step. Tell me, please, tell me.

HELEN. I'm really fine, this is an exaggeration.

BECCA. Mum /

HELEN. Yesterday was not good but it won't happen again, it was a one-off.

BECCA. Mum, please.

HELEN. I'll ring work, I'll apologise, I'm sure they'll understand it was a one /

BECCA. Mum.

HELEN. I'm fine, Becca.

–

–

BECCA. Okay. Okay well I'm sorry I can't do this any more. I can't see you any more.

15.

HELEN. Thank you for agreeing to meet me.

BECCA. It's okay.

HELEN. You look /

BECCA. Yeah.

HELEN. Nice hair /

BECCA. Thank you.

HELEN. Is that a new watch /

BECCA. No. Well, last year, Dave got it for my birthday /

HELEN. Right, well that's, that's lovely. Really beautiful.

BECCA. Thanks.

HELEN. Did you get my card?

BECCA. Yes.

HELEN. I'm sorry I couldn't, I thought you wouldn't want me to / come

BECCA. You were right.

HELEN. I'm doing much better. I really am doing much much better.

BECCA. You said in the card.

HELEN. I'm going to some meetings, and I've been talking to

people, I've been /

BECCA. Good.

HELEN. It's so lovely to see you.

–

I've missed you.

–

I'm sorry I didn't, I'm sorry I didn't let you help, I'm sorry
I didn't admit it, I wasn't ready I couldn't –

BECCA. Okay.

HELEN. But I have now. I have now and I'm just here to say
I'm doing much better.

I joined a salsa class –

Not that that's why I'm doing much better, just saying I'm
doing things you know, to try and, new things not just home
alone, yeah, sorry –

I really miss you and I know you're angry but I'd really love
it if we could –

If we could, just go back to how –

Or even, forward, to something, because I need you and I'm
sorry for not admitting I was, for getting lost in that well
of loneliness and not letting you pull me out. I'm sorry for
leaving you there on your own.

–

BECCA. I've missed you too.

HELEN. Yes?

BECCA. Of course, yes. I just want you to be happy, Mum.

HELEN. Me too, me too and I'm trying to get there I really am.

16.

BECCA. I wanted to tell you first /

HELEN. That's incredible /

BECCA. We're not really telling other people yet so if you could /

HELEN. Of course, yeah of course /

BECCA. It's a bit early but I just wanted you to know.

HELEN. I'm so happy, fuck I'm so, that's just wonderful.

BECCA. Yes.

HELEN. You're, I mean you're happy right, you wanted /

BECCA. Yeah we both wanted.

HELEN. That's amazing.

BECCA. Thanks, Mum.

HELEN. I can't believe it /

BECCA. You'll be a grandma.

HELEN. I will not be a grandma.

BECCA. Okay.

HELEN. Or a nana.

BECCA. Grandmother is pretty formal.

HELEN. I'll be Helen. I'll be their favourite Helen.

BECCA. Okay, Mum.

HELEN. I tried to make you call me Helen.

BECCA. I remember.

HELEN. Yes it didn't really catch on.

BECCA. No.

HELEN. Oh, Becca, this is just /

BECCA. Yeah.

HELEN. I wish, I wish your dad could've /

BECCA. Me too.

HELEN. Yeah. He would've made a great grandad.

BECCA. Yeah.

HELEN. Oh god, I'm, cry at everything now, it's age.

BECCA. Mum.

HELEN. No they're happy tears, they are, I'm happy, I'm so
happy for you.

BECCA. Thank you.

HELEN. You're going to be a wonderful mum.

BECCA. You're going to be the best Helen.

HELEN. I hope so. I really hope so.

17.

BECCA. It's a girl.

Yeah. Yeah. A girl.

I know, but, Dave was there. We didn't want everyone to –

Yes. Okay. Pretty sore. But nothing, nothing too bad.

I lost a bit of blood. We're staying in overnight. But they said
it should be fine.

No honestly they said /

A girl, yes, I know.

Seven pounds.

Evie. Evie we think.

I know. I know I can't wait either.

18.

BECCA. You didn't have to come.

HELEN. I know.

BECCA. I didn't mean you had to drop everything and just come.

HELEN. I know that, it's fine, I wanted to.

BECCA. I think this will probably pass.

HELEN. Are you eating?

BECCA. Mum /

HELEN. Are you?

BECCA. Yes, sort of, yes, it's, it's not that. It's not always that.

HELEN. Have you spoken to anyone else?

BECCA. It's probably just fleeting, just with Dave back at work –

It's just yesterday I felt a little, it can be you know –

HELEN. Overwhelming /

BECCA. Numbing.

HELEN. Just yesterday?

BECCA. No. For a while now.

HELEN. Does David know?

BECCA. He does, he's so good, with her and with everything he's so /

HELEN. Yes.

BECCA. He's so good I'm not sure he really gets it you know.

HELEN. Okay.

BECCA. I'm not sure I really get it. This is, my husband and my baby, beautiful baby and I should be so happy so perfect, I should be –

HELEN. You're doing great. It's totally normal to be floored.

BECCA. It's just, I didn't expect it to feel so much like /

HELEN. Exhaustion.

BECCA. Grief.

HELEN. Oh.

BECCA. Is that a really weird thing to say?

HELEN. No, love.

BECCA. I feel like that's such a fucking weird thing to say.

HELEN. It's bound to stir things up.

BECCA. Sometimes I look at her, and I just, I don't know, I can't feel anything.

HELEN. Right.

BECCA. Is that, I don't know is that normal?

HELEN. I'm, I'm not sure /

BECCA. And sometimes I look at her and I feel so responsible, I feel so scared something will happen to her, I feel certain that something will happen to her and I won't stop it.

HELEN. You're doing an amazing job.

BECCA. I think I might be going mad.

HELEN. Have you been getting any sleep?

BECCA. The other day I looked at her in the bathroom and I just knew she was an angel. I just knew she was an angel and that I shouldn't touch her, none of us should touch her because we might not do it right.

That's crazy, isn't it?

HELEN. You're just, lots of people struggle after birth.

BECCA. This should be the happiest time of my, me and Dave and our baby, it should be the happiest time of, and I know I love her. I know it but I can't always feel it you know. I can't always feel me.

HELEN. You need to talk to someone.

BECCA. I felt like this when Dad died.

HELEN. Yes, love.

BECCA. I didn't think, I mean having a baby shouldn't feel –

HELEN. It doesn't matter what it should feel. It matters what you feel.

BECCA. I'm a terrible mum. Already. She's only two months old and I'm already terrible.

HELEN. You are not.

BECCA. I am.

HELEN. No you're not, you're really not. Okay. Becca? Okay.

BECCA. Okay.

HELEN. I was really scared when you were born.

BECCA. Were you?

HELEN. Yes. Yes I was fucking terrified okay. And I fucked it up, a lot. I dropped you, and gave you rashes, and panicked when you were sick and the first time I had to give you a bath I locked us in the bathroom and cried because I thought I might drown you.

BECCA. Okay. Yeah okay but this feels /

HELEN. Yes. So being nervous and tired and overwhelmed and almost grieving this massive change you are going through at the same time, at the same time as being happy and grateful and in love with this new perfect creature that's all normal /

BECCA. Yes but this, I feel, this is –

HELEN. Yes. This could be more, maybe, who knows. We'll talk to your health visitor. We'll ring them. They know about these things more now, it's not uncommon.

BECCA. Okay.

HELEN. It's not your fault.

BECCA. Okay.

HELEN. Becca? It's not okay?

BECCA. Okay.

19.

HELEN. Gosh she looks just like you.

BECCA. She doesn't.

HELEN. She does, those little pigtails and that miniature uniform.

BECCA. She hates those pigtails but I'm not having her get nits.

HELEN. Honestly she's the spitting image, I've got a picture somewhere of you like that with Dad.

BECCA. I've never seen it.

HELEN. You must have, years ago, you must have.

BECCA. I haven't.

HELEN. I definitely used to have one, I'll find it. Same little cheeky grin.

BECCA. That must seem like a long time ago.

HELEN. Feels like yesterday.

BECCA. Years.

HELEN. You'll think the same on her soon enough.

BECCA. It's hard, isn't it /

HELEN. What?

BECCA. First day, sending her off. I don't know how you did it.

HELEN. Glad to get you out the front door, get a break.

BECCA. Charming.

HELEN. No, no it is hard. So small, I remember thinking you were so small to be starting the day on your own.

BECCA. Yes.

HELEN. With your packed lunch.

BECCA. Cheese and pickle.

HELEN. Yep.

BECCA. Pickle to be scraped off and binned.

HELEN. I never knew that.

BECCA. I always asked you not to put it in.

HELEN. Did you?

BECCA. Yes.

HELEN. I don't remember, sorry.

BECCA. She's having school meals.

HELEN. Right.

BECCA. They're nice now, not like when I was there. No chocolate concrete in sight.

HELEN. That is a shame.

BECCA. Maybe.

HELEN. I'm so proud of her.

BECCA. Yeah. This morning I just I looked at her and I –

He'll never meet her. Do you ever think that?

Sometimes, like this morning she's doing something and I think he would have loved that and he'll never get to know. Does that ever /

HELEN. All the time.

BECCA. I think he would have found her funny.

HELEN. They would have been a pair. They would have been terrors.

BECCA. Yeah. Yeah anyway I just popped round to see if you're still okay to pick her up tomorrow.

HELEN. Absolutely.

BECCA. Dave's at work and with it being my first day.

HELEN. Of course, I love to have her you know that.

BECCA. Thanks, Mum.

HELEN. She's such a bright little thing, she's going to do well.

BECCA. I hope so.

HELEN. Just like you.

20.

HELEN. Are you sure?

BECCA. I'm really sure.

HELEN. And with Evie, what will?

BECCA. We're going to share, we've got an arrangement, Tuesday and Wednesday evenings, alternate weekends.

HELEN. That sounds, practical.

BECCA. Yes.

HELEN. Are you okay?

BECCA. I'm fine.

HELEN. Really, really are you okay?

BECCA. Yes.

HELEN. Okay. Okay well great.

BECCA. I know you were never that keen on him /

HELEN. I've always liked David.

BECCA. Mum /

HELEN. I have, I have, I've never said /

BECCA. No you've never said. But /

HELEN. What?

BECCA. Nothing. I'm just saying this isn't, it's very civil, we
    still care for each other a lot, so I just want us all to be /

HELEN. Of course.

BECCA. Okay.

    –

HELEN. Was it /

BECCA. My idea.

HELEN. Okay.

BECCA. I mean we discussed it together but I /

HELEN. Yes. And was there anything that, sparked it, that /

BECCA. Not really.

HELEN. Okay.

BECCA. No one's cheated on anyone if that's what you mean.

HELEN. No no, I wouldn't think, David's always been very,
    solid.

BECCA. Solid?

HELEN. I just mean I wouldn't have thought either of you had /

BECCA. Okay.

HELEN. Yes.

BECCA. Solid. That's a good thing.

HELEN. Yes.

BECCA. You don't make it seem like a good thing.

HELEN. It is, I meant, it is definitely /

BECCA. Solid. Like boring.

HELEN. I, I think you're putting words in my mouth.

BECCA. Okay.

HELEN. I'm sorry for both of you, I'm sorry. I'm not gloating
or anything, I hope you're okay.

BECCA. Okay.

HELEN. Becca?

BECCA. Yes. Okay.

–

–

I suppose I, I suppose I, after Dad and uni and everything,
solid was what, is what I want you know. It's just it hasn't,
for us it –

You know we were going out to dinner last week and I was
nervous. Nervous. We live together for god's sake but I was
nervous we were going to have to spend an hour together
without the TV or work or Evie or anyone else. I was nervous
we wouldn't have anything to say.

HELEN. Well that's /

BECCA. And I was right. Because we didn't.

HELEN. If you know then you know, darling.

BECCA. Not all of us can be you two I suppose /

HELEN. Us two?

BECCA. You and Dad.

HELEN. Just because he's dead doesn't mean we have to
worship him, Becca. I love him, loved him but he was an
arse.

BECCA. Mum /

HELEN. If he was still alive, us, who knows.

BECCA. But you've never, I mean you've never with anyone else /

HELEN. So you think.

BECCA. What does that mean?

HELEN. I realised pretty early on from your reaction you weren't going to take anything too well /

BECCA. That's not fair.

HELEN. Isn't it?

BECCA. I, I don't know.

–

HELEN. I might have a *friend* /

BECCA. What?

HELEN. He comes round on Wednesdays and Fridays /

BECCA. Mum.

HELEN. And has done for a while.

BECCA. That's, well that's –

If I've stopped you, from moving on, from, you know having a proper relationship /

HELEN. You haven't stopped me from anything. This is, this is just right for me. Freedom. My life. Your dad was, he took up a lot of space, didn't he, in all our hearts, lives and god love him I'm wasn't prepared to give that space up again.

BECCA. Okay, so /

HELEN. Okay, so. This works for me, and in time you're going to find something that works for you.

BECCA. Right.

–

HELEN. You're allowed to be sad, Becca, even if it was your decision, you're allowed to be upset.

BECCA. I'll bear that in mind.

HELEN. I hope you will.

21.

BECCA. They're lovely flowers.

HELEN. Oh they're nothing.

BECCA. I don't know how you got out to get them.

HELEN. Well I might have enlisted our little helper.

BECCA. Oh I see.

HELEN. She's a sweetheart.

BECCA. She's a madam.

HELEN. Not to me.

BECCA. No, that's true.

HELEN. Everyone's a madam at her age.

BECCA. I wasn't /

HELEN. I'm not so sure.

—

BECCA. Has Lisa been across today?

HELEN. Tuesdays and Thursdays are her day.

BECCA. I wish you'd let me get someone in more often.

HELEN. You're here.

BECCA. What if you fell.

HELEN. Then I'd get back up.

BECCA. What if you couldn't /

HELEN. I'm not a child.

BECCA. Mum /

HELEN. Not today, eh, Becca.

BECCA. Okay.

–

HELEN. You doing anything special?

BECCA. Oh I'm not sure.

HELEN. Nothing?

BECCA. Well, maybe I'll meet some people for a drink later?

HELEN. Oh, very nice.

BECCA. David's got Evie so /

HELEN. Right of course.

–

Are you okay?

BECCA. Me?

HELEN. Yes. You look –

BECCA. What?

HELEN. Nothing, just you look, you don't look okay.

BECCA. Thanks.

HELEN. You look tired.

BECCA. That means old.

HELEN. No, you just. Your eyes, just, a bit tired maybe.

BECCA. Old.

HELEN. I didn't say that.

BECCA. On my birthday. Kick me when I'm down.

HELEN. I never said old. I'm just checking you're okay.

BECCA. I'm fine.

HELEN. Have you been eating?

BECCA. Mum /

HELEN. Have you?

BECCA. I'm a grown woman.

HELEN. You still need to eat.

BECCA. I'm fine.

HELEN. Are you?

BECCA. It's you we worry about now.

HELEN. So you seem to think.

–

BECCA. Do you think it's weird, this, I mean on the run up to it did it feel weird?

HELEN. What?

BECCA. My, you know, my birthday.

HELEN. Your birthday?

BECCA. I'm older now than he ever was.

HELEN. Oh. That.

BECCA. I'm his daughter, but I'm older than him.

HELEN. Yes.

BECCA. That feels –

HELEN. Yes.

BECCA. We've lived more of life without him than we did together.

HELEN. Yes. Yes we have.

–

BECCA. I wanted to say sorry.

HELEN. Don't be stupid.

BECCA. No, I did, I wanted to say sorry. For all the, because
when Dad died it felt like to me, it felt, it was sad but he was
old, in my mind he was old and so were you and it's only
now I'm here I can see how much you had left –

HELEN. It's okay –

BECCA. I don't think I understood that very well. What that
was like, when you still could have had so much together.
I don't think I understood that very well. I'm sorry.

HELEN. It's okay. I think you did pretty well. I think we both
did okay, didn't we?

BECCA. I hope so.

HELEN. So these drinks you might go for tonight, just with
a friend, are they?

BECCA. What's that supposed to mean?

HELEN. Just asking. I've heard you mention Steve from work,
a few times, I just wondered /

BECCA. Maybe.

HELEN. I knew it, you love a man whose name screams
overalls.

BECCA. Mum!

HELEN. That's great, Becca, that's really great.

BECCA. It's nothing serious you know /

HELEN. You deserve to have fun /

BECCA. Evie doesn't like it.

HELEN. No, no she won't. I remember that.

BECCA. Okay, okay point taken.

HELEN. Cuppa?

BECCA. I'll get it. You stay sat down.

HELEN. I can still boil a kettle.

BECCA. I worry about your hands.

HELEN. You worry too much.

BECCA. Maybe. But I'll still do it.

22.

BECCA. It's not a home.

HELEN. So you say.

BECCA. Retirement community.

HELEN. Right.

BECCA. It's really nice, the gardens /

HELEN. I see.

BECCA. It just means that we don't have to worry, because there's always someone on hand to check. So if anything were to happen /

HELEN. I've got a phone here.

BECCA. Yes, Mum, but that's only, I mean if you're conscious, what if you fall, or if you don't remember /

HELEN. I remember /

BECCA. Mostly.

HELEN. I don't know how I'd afford it.

BECCA. We'd sell your flat.

HELEN. I love my flat.

BECCA. Yes, Mum, but the stairs now, and layout. It's not very practical. What if a carer needed to stay?

HELEN. I don't need a carer.

BECCA. Not yet but –

HELEN. Are you asking me or telling me this?

BECCA. You get your own space there, it's not like a home, you can join in as much or as little as you like, I'm not saying you suddenly have to join the WI and start knitting /

HELEN. Aren't you?

BECCA. Everything else can stay just the same, the rest of your life it would just mean we knew /

HELEN. Someone was keeping an eye.

BECCA. Yes.

HELEN. Yes.

23.

BECCA. Mum?

HELEN. What?

BECCA. I was just saying we might take you out, tomorrow. If you're feeling up for it.

HELEN. Who?

BECCA. Me. Maybe Evie too. We've got the wheelchair and it's meant to be nice weather.

HELEN. I don't know who that girl is.

BECCA. She works here, Mum, It's Lucy, you remember. She's just changing your sheets.

HELEN. She doesn't knock.

BECCA. She does knock, Mum.

HELEN. I've not been feeling very well.

BECCA. I know, Mum. I know, but you look a bit better today.

HELEN. You haven't been to see me.

BECCA. I have, I've been every day.

HELEN. You haven't.

BECCA. Okay.

—

Would you like to do that tomorrow?

HELEN. What?

BECCA. Come out. With me and Evie? It's Dad's anniversary, isn't it? And I thought we could go to the park, like we sometimes do? To the ducks? You know like we used to do.

HELEN. He hasn't been to see me once, you know.

BECCA. Who, Mum?

HELEN. Your dad. I keep waiting for him but he hasn't been.

BECCA. Mum, Dad's not, not for a long time now, has he? You remember.

HELEN. A good-looking man your dad, isn't he? Too good looking, some might say, but he's never been gone like his.

BECCA. Okay, Mum.

HELEN. I haven't been out of here, they won't let me, she won't let me get out of here.

BECCA. We're going to go out tomorrow, Mum.

HELEN. She won't let me do anything, they watch me you know.

BECCA. Mum /

HELEN. Where?

BECCA. What?

HELEN. Tomorrow. Where are we going to go?

BECCA. To the park, Mum. We're going to go to one of your favourite spots.

24. The End

BECCA. Evie.

EVIE. I'm coming. Hold on.

BECCA. We made it.

EVIE. I'm knackered.

BECCA. God. Look. It looks just like it did all those years ago.

EVIE. Yeah?

BECCA. We should have come back, maybe. We should have come back more.

EVIE. We should do this quick before it rains.

BECCA. Yes.

EVIE. You okay?

BECCA. I feel a bit –

EVIE. I know /

BECCA. Sweaty, it's quite a climb.

EVIE. It is.

BECCA. Still, if it was clear the view would be just –

EVIE. Yeah.

BECCA. It's nice to think that he's been here, all this time.

   Okay. Okay, I'm ready, are you ready?

EVIE. I've got you.

BECCA. I've got a technique this time, I've even brought gloves but it's not raining.

EVIE. We should say something.

BECCA. Yeah.

EVIE. Yeah.

BECCA. Okay. Okay, god this is hard –

EVIE. You can do it.

BECCA. Bye. We love you. We –

I hope you know that, knew that, I hope you –

Because there's something I said once, when I was angry –

There was something I said to you I didn't mean and I've never –

I just want to tell you –

I'm glad it wasn't you. I'm so so glad.

–

Okay. Okay Bye. Bye, Mum.

EVIE. Bye, Grandma.

BECCA. Helen.

EVIE. Bye, Helen.

BECCA. We love you.

EVIE. We really love you.

BECCA. Ahooohhhhhaaaaa.

–

–

EVIE. Look at that.

BECCA. The clouds are sort of clearing.

EVIE. Yeah, who'd have thought it.

BECCA. I can almost see the sun.

EVIE. Don't go too far.

BECCA. Almost.

–

God it really is amazing up here, isn't it? The view. The view when it's not raining.

EVIE. It will soon.

BECCA. I see what he meant.

EVIE. Who?

BECCA. *I could live here.*

EVIE. You'd be cold.

BECCA. Maybe.

EVIE. Come on, Mum.

BECCA. Yeah, yeah okay, I'm coming.

A Nick Hern Book

Helen first published in Great Britain as a paperback original in 2023 by Nick Hern Books Limited, The Glasshouse, 49a Goldhawk Road, London W12 8QP, in association with Terrain and Theatre503

Helen copyright © 2023 Maureen Lennon

Maureen Lennon has asserted her right to be identified as the author of this work

Cover design by Studio Blue Creative

Designed and typeset by Nick Hern Books, London
Printed in Great Britain by Mimeo Ltd, Huntingdon, Cambridgeshire PE29 6XX

A CIP catalogue record for this book is available from the British Library

ISBN 978 1 83904 247 8